SELL

YOUR SHOW

IN SECONDS

How to
create crowd-pulling
publicity materials for
more ticket sales and less stress

OLIVER MEECH

For my family.

CONTENTS

Intro 7

Educational 13

Creating your show image 21

Stand out 41

Tempting 53

Personal 63

Simple 77

Beyond posters 89

Yes, but… 93

Outro 97

Spread the word 99

Acknowledgements 101

Get in touch 103

Appendix – useful resources 105

INTRO

If I could sum up my experience of preparing shows for fringe festivals in one word, it would be this:

Aaargh!

Aaargh, how am I going to make an hour of good stuff in a matter of months?

Aaargh, how can a simple show cost so much to stage?

Aaargh, how-is-it-a-month-to-go-already?

Essentially, aaargh – too much to do in too little time.

And unless you're already a superstar with a crack PR posse, you can add to this:
Aaargh, what should I do about my poster and flyers?

What should my image be? How can I communicate a whole show in just a few seconds? And how can I compete with all the other shows vying for attention?

I feel your pain. And while I can't make the process of preparing a show entirely stress-free, I can hopefully make it a lot easier to create good posters and flyers. Maybe even great ones.

And while they can't single-handedly turn your show into a hot ticket, they can help to:

- Clarify your show in potential punters' minds (and your own)
- Look professional (even if you don't feel it)
- Intrigue the press, who need interesting images to fill their festival content
- Give your PR (if you have one) something to send on
- Make it easier for your flyerers (if you're using them) to sell your show, as your flyer does a lot of the selling for them
- Improve the odds of your flyers being kept, so you're less likely to watch, heartbroken, as someone drops your flyer on the floor and the person behind them treads on your tiny face (not that it's ever happened to me, no no, of course not, just saying, y'know, theoretically, if it did… *starts twitching*)
- Make your show easier to remember and to choose
- Swiftly sum up your show for touring venues
- Make you feel more in control while you're riding the fringe rollercoaster

Who am I?

For the last fifteen years or so I've juggled two careers, as a Magician and an Advertising Creative (i.e. someone who creates ideas and writes ads). As the former, I've had two sell-out runs at the Edinburgh Fringe, and toured my show to theatres and venues across the UK. As the latter, I've worked at some of the world's biggest agencies, advertising some of the world's best-known brands, including Amazon, Heineken, Sky, Tesco, Nando's, National Lottery and the NHS, picking up a few awards along the way. If you've watched it, worn it, or eaten it, there's a good chance I've created ads for it. On an average week in advertising, I'll create anywhere between 15 to 150 ideas for ads (no exaggeration), so I've created literally hundreds, if not thousands, of posters and press ads over the years.

It's given me an interesting perspective on show posters (and other promotional materials). I've noticed that many of them aren't working as effectively as they could. Quite often I can see some simple tweaks that would instantly make them more captivating and compelling. While I've been able to give some people individual advice, there's a limit to how many performers I can speak with. So I've decided to capture my thinking on paper and this is the result.

Who is this book for?

This book is aimed at two types of people. Primarily, it's for those who are new to making posters. Perhaps you're creating your first one, or you've made one that was disappointing and you're looking for ways to improve the next. If so, the suggestions in this book will help you create a better poster, faster, while avoiding many of the common mistakes that I've made along the way.

Secondly, it's for those who have made a few posters but are looking for some fresh perspectives. If that's you, then you'll find some more tools for your creative tool box, and some simple ways to make a good poster even better.

My focus will mostly be on having a good idea for your poster, for two reasons. It's the part that many people skip, or don't spend enough time on. And it's the foundation that makes everything else easier – get the idea right and the rest will follow.

With a good idea, you don't have to rely on your photographer working wonders with lighting, or your designer having a flash of inspiration. Your poster will already contain the elements you need to grab attention, help people understand your show quickly, and convert more potential punters into audience members. It also makes the process of producing your poster a lot less stressful. And, since I've never heard a performer say "I'm bored. All my prep's sorted and there's still six months to go", anything that makes the process quicker and more painless can only be a good thing.

Finally, once you have a good poster, it's relatively easy to adapt it into a flyer, social media post, or whatever else you need. I'll generally talk about posters, because 'promotional materials' is a bit of a mouthful, but most of the principles can be applied to everything.

How to use this book

This book is a step-by-step guide to making, and improving, a poster. That said, while I'd recommend reading it from start to finish, if you're short of time and have a particular area that needs sorting (e.g. your poster feels cluttered so you're looking for ways to simplify it) then by all means skip straight to that section. And if, like House of Pain, you just love to jump around, then do that. As with most things in life, do what works for you.

The road ahead

Here's a rough route map of your quest for poster glory:

Generally, you'll take a series of steps to create your poster, in order to maximise its pulling power. I mean that both literally, and figuratively because STEPS is an acronym. It reminds you to make your poster Simple, Tempting, Educational, Personal and Stand-out. We'll actually be applying them in a slightly different order, but ESTPS isn't as catchy.

More specifically, you'll start by making the concept of your show as clear (Educational) as possible.

Next, you'll use a range of techniques to brainstorm ideas for an interesting show image, then use some helpful criteria to select the best one(s) to progress.

After that, you'll tweak your poster to make it more Stand-out, Tempting, Personal and Simple.

Then, you'll move onto adapting it to other types of media (e.g. flyers, online ads, etc.).

And finally, you'll get some suggestions for what to do if you find yourself in a pickle.

If you follow the principles in this book, you should end up producing a poster to be proud of. I can't guarantee that you'll also have a sell-out show, but you will put the odds forever in your favour, like the Hunger Games (but without all that messy killing).

Right, enough preamble – I've written (and rewritten) this book to boil it down to the essentials, so you get the maximum advice in the minimum time. Because we've all got too much to do. Let's jump in.

EDUCATIONAL

What's the primary goal of promotional posters and flyers?

To look cool? Nope, that's design.

To express your vision? Nope, that's art.

It's not even to get people to see your show – that's the secondary goal.

The primary goal is to communicate. It's the first thing I was taught on my advertising course back when I was a fresh-faced graduate, and it's still just as true over a decade later.

Your mission is to communicate.

It sounds obvious, yet I've seen countless posters and flyers that leave me none the wiser. Often the ones with the longest blurbs end up telling me the least.

It's amazing how few shows shift their focus from their

own point of view to that of their potential punters. But it's completely understandable – we're so close to our shows that it's hard to see them objectively.

It reminds me of an orange juice carton I once saw on holiday, which had a photo of its vast metal factory splashed across one side. Sure, the company were proud of it, but why should we, the audience, care? We'd probably rather see something like, well, an orange.

So, how do you find out what your audience want to know, without a giant therapist's couch? Thankfully, it's simple. I'll tell you. When considering a show, potential punters want answers to these three questions:

1. What is it?
2. Is it any good?
3. Can I go?

That's pretty much it. Give them what they need to answer those three things and you stand a good chance of them coming.

And what are you aiming for in your answers?

Clarity.

It beats everything else. You can't guarantee that people will want to see your show, but you can make it quick and easy for them to make an informed choice.

You may think that by keeping it vague then you avoid putting anyone off, but in fact vagueness leads to uncertainty, and if people don't know what they're getting, then they generally don't get it!

It's easy to try and sell the show to everyone, but as the saying goes, if you try and appeal to everyone, you'll end up appealing to no-one.

Mid-way through my first fringe, I remember getting frustrated at the people who instantly dismissed the idea of seeing a magic show. After all, I thought in my neurotic-yet-egotistical-artist's way, 'Who wouldn't love my show?!'. Then I finished flyering for the day and was offered a flyer for a tragic opera sung entirely in German. Now, it doesn't matter how good it is, tragic opera just doesn't do it for me, especially when it's in a language I've always struggled with (despite the best efforts of my high school German teacher). It made me realise that some people feel the same way about magic, and that's ok. It helped me take rejection less personally.

So, we'll start by answering the first question – what is it?

Rather than staring at a white page, you're going to create a basic poster in five minutes as a starting point. Because, to quote Jodi Picoult: You can always edit a bad page. You can't edit a blank page.

The solid start

Let's knock up a standard poster.

Grab a piece of white paper and a pen and fill in the following, from the top of the page down:

- YOUR NAME
- YOUR SHOW TITLE
- YOUR IMAGE: draw a stick-person head facing front as a placeholder
- YOUR SUPPORTING QUOTE(S): if you don't have any, just put 'it's incredible' by Joe Bloggs
- YOUR EVENT'S DATE AND TIME
- YOUR VENUE

- YOUR VENUE/FRINGE FESTIVAL LOGO (IF NEEDED)

Congratulations! You have a poster. It seems simple, and it is. Yes, it's currently a bit blah but it has all the elements it needs to communicate. Now we can make more of each element, to create a properly kickass poster.

Clear posters come from clear shows

Now, your show concept is probably one of three things: it's clear, it's a bit muddled, or it's non-existent.

If your concept is clear…

Then this is ideal. If you can design the show from the start to be easily-sum-up-able (without destroying your artistic vision) then it will make designing your promotional materials much easier.

If your concept is a bit muddled…

Then it's probably because it contains a few different aspects. In this case, list the different aspects of the show, then pick one (or a few) to highlight. This could be the dominant aspect, what you think is most interesting to your audience, or what's most distinctive from other shows. If you worked in advertising, you'd call this the 'strategy', 'positioning' or 'proposition'. If you worked in journalism, it would be the 'angle' or 'hook'. But since you don't, you don't have to call it anything!

You see Hollywood doing the same thing. For instance, back when Tim Burton's *Sweeney Todd* came out, the trailer led on the story, the stars and the director, and left out the small but important fact that it was also a musical. Thankfully, we don't need to go to that extreme.

After all, audiences rarely enjoy a bait-and-switch.

If your concept is non-existent...

Then don't despair. Not all shows need concepts, and many do very well without one – most mixed-bill shows, for instance. Here are four ways forward:

1. Play off yourself as a performer, rather than your show. This works particularly well if you have a strong, clear persona (see the 'Personal' chapter later)

2. Give a broad feel for the type of show it is (e.g. comedy, theatre, dance), ideally supported with good reviews (see the 'Tempting' chapter later).

3. Stand out through a playful title, or visual. As the song says, it ain't what you do, it's the way that you do it. For example, dynamic magical duo Griffin and Jones call one of their shows *Trickorice Allsorts* (a play on Liquorice Allsorts, a British sweet), which is much more interesting than something meh like *The Magic Variety Show*.

4. Revel in its lack of concept – highlight the absence of a big unwieldy theme, as the superb Stuart Goldsmith did with his show *An hour*.

Example

Let's take a hypothetical example of a slightly muddled show concept and see what our hook could be. We'll imagine the show is a devised student drama, with songs and poetry, about a group of university friends who pontificate about the meaning of life and death. The title is *Ephemeral*, which was hastily chosen to hit the programme deadline, months before the show was actually developed.

So, what hook do we use for this multi-faceted, slightly woolly show? It's a tricky one. As is often the case, there's no one right answer. So here are nine possible approaches to take, which you can also apply to your own show, to help people get the show quickly:

1. *Comparing it to something they know and love:*
   If you liked *The Breakfast Club* then you'll like this.

2. *Describing it as a combination of two existing things:*
   It's *Eat Pray Love* meets *8 Mile*.

3. *Making a jokey comparison to an existing show:*
   It's like *Mamma Mia*, but with less ABBA and more death.

4. *Making a bold claim:*
   Discover the meaning of life in 55 minutes.

5. *Being nostalgic:*
   Relive university without the hangover.

6. *Asking an intriguing question:*
   What's the worst life choice you've ever made?

7. *Pitching it as good value:*
   See 3 shows for the price of 1: part play, part musical, part slam poetry.

8. *Embracing its uniqueness:*
   It's like nothing you've ever seen.
   (A Facebook ad for *Pluto* at the Barbican used the excellent term 'genre-defying').

9. *Distinguishing it from the majority of other shows:*
   Warning: does not contain stand-up.

Now it's your turn. Take the nine approaches, and see if you can come up with a line, or ideally multiple lines, for each one. Start by generating as many as possible, without any filtering. To quote *My Name Is Earl*: don't be judging. Aim for quantity, then you can sift for quality afterwards.

There's another benefit to coming up with loads of lines. You can use one as your main hook and keep the others for use in your show blurb and press release. You can also keep a few in mind for flyering, especially if you find that some lines work better for certain types of people (e.g. families, locals, sailors, goat-herders).

Get it? Got it. Good!

The result of all this thinking is that you now have a way for people to get your show in moments. Well done, you've moved potential punters one step closer to buying a ticket. Now you've found a way to clearly summarise your show concept, you're in a good place to dramatise it with your show image.

CREATING YOUR SHOW IMAGE

If you feel like you already have a genius idea for your show image then feel free to skip this section. Although, even if you do, it's still worth exploring other ideas before leaping into production. Sometimes in advertising, my first 'unbeatable' idea has been rejected for some reason and I've had to come up with another one, sharpish. Often, this second idea ends up being better than the first. For the sake of an extra hour, you may as well brainstorm some more options. You can always revert to your initial image afterwards if you still prefer it.

If, as is more likely, you haven't been struck by divine inspiration, don't worry. You don't need to wait for the muse (see 'Forget Your Muse' on *Copyblogger*), you can rely on a few tried and true techniques to give you a better chance of coming up with a something really good.

Storming it: generating ideas

Ok, it's time to brainstorm. While there's no magic secret to having a great idea (sadly), there are several techniques that definitely help. I've outlined each of them below. Most of them aren't original with me, but they've proved very useful whenever I've had a blank page and a looming deadline.

Don't aim for 'great', aim for 'lots'

You can't guarantee your first idea will be great. Or your second. Perhaps only one in ten will be good. And one in 50 will be great. So, if you only come up with one idea, you're not giving yourself the best chance of creating something remarkable.

Thankfully, the reverse is also true. If you come up with 50 ideas, you should end up with five good ideas to choose from. Quantity breeds quality.

I realise that coming up with loads of ideas can seem a bit daunting, so here are a bunch of ways to help you become a Lean Mean Creating Machine (or a Plump Kind Creating Machine, your choice).

Create now, judge later

This is one of the most important tips, yet one of the hardest to follow. For some reason, creative people are often highly self-critical (myself included). There are some benefits to this, as you need to have high standards to make an excellent show. But if you start judging as you go, it seriously slows your flow of ideas.

Start by brain dumping all the ideas you can think of onto the page with no judging or editing – even if they seem 'silly' or 'wrong' (in fact, especially if they're 'silly' or 'wrong'). Don't 'over think' it, just fill the page. You can always filter them later.

Give yourself a set period of time to brainstorm – I find bursts of around 20-40 minutes work well. It's enough time to explore several different avenues, without it becoming a mental marathon.

Draw scamps

I was very confused when I started working in advertising and heard people talking about scamps. What was this mystical thing? A type of stamp? A small insect? A cheeky child? Turns out it just means a rough sketch of an ad.

Making a quick drawing of your ad can really help you to clarify your ideas – it gets them out of your head and down on paper, where you can play around with them or show them to others. It also allows you to try a lot of different ideas quickly, without wasting hours polishing each one.

Don't worry if you can't draw well – I can't either. My skills are still at the stick-person level. In fact, not being able to draw well can be a benefit, as it forces you to make your idea really clear and easy to convey. In general, if an image it too complex to be able to be easily drawn, then it's too complex. That said, if you're really struggling, then there's no shame in tracing outlines of objects or people off the internet.

Write down everything

It's easy to think that you'll remember everything, but in practice you won't, so scribble down every thought. For the same reason, keep a notebook by your bed for any 3am ideas, and consider taking one with you in case you have any brainwaves when you're going about your day. Alternatively, use your phone notes app – just make sure it automatically backs up, so you don't literally lose your mind if you lose your phone.

Start with your brain, not the internet ('You-gle' before you Google!)

I know it's tempting to Google the subject of your show and scroll through images for inspiration. But try to hold off, at least until you've had an initial splurge yourself, for these three reasons:

1. Everyone else who Googles the subject will see similar images.

2. Your brain thinks in a more unique way than a computer, and has more individual connections with other ideas, so use your uniqueness first. You may think up an image that's never been done before, whereas if you search online, by definition you can only develop something with a precedent.

3. You may end up doing something because you fall in love with a particular image, rather than because it's the best encapsulation of your show.

But Google's great once you have an idea

That's not to say that Googling images can't be helpful. Once you have an idea that you've drawn a scribbly scamp for, and you're looking to brief a photographer or designer, then looking for reference images of similar styles can be very helpful. It's a lot easier to show the shade of blue you'd like than to try and describe it as "like the love-child of a blueberry and a peacock". Rather than a single image, try to find a few, to make a 'mood board'. This way, you can be influenced by other images without directly duplicating them. (This idea is covered in more detail in *Steal Like An Artist* by Austin Kleon).

Think on paper

A great way to increase your quantity of ideas is to write them down. It frees up your working memory from remembering your ideas, so you can focus on creating more of them.

My favourite way to think on paper is to brainstorm by drawing mind maps (aka spider diagrams). Personally, I use an A3 pad of plain paper, laid sideways (landscape). It gives you enough space to explore several different areas, without being too big and unwieldy. But if you prefer a small notebook then go with that. There are even brainstorming apps, though I find they slow me down, and their neater nature makes me shy of putting down all my ideas, however scrappy. There's no one perfect way to create – just experiment and find what works for you.

Assuming you're using a pad, write the name of the show in the centre, circle it, then add about 10 rays coming out from it, like a scribbly sun. Thanks to your brain's cravings for completeness, just having those lines radiating out will encourage you to fill them with ideas.

Now just start throwing out any images and associations that spring to mind. If your show combines two main concepts, then you can draw two main lines, then have further offshoots from each, so you end up with a diagram which resembles a tree. Brainstorm a load of associations for each concept, then you can think about different ways to combine them afterwards.

Other angles to explore when brainstorming

Contrast

This is another powerful and flexible way to make posters. In fact, contrast is one of the four principles of design often taught to new designers (for more on that, check out *The Non-Designer's Design Book* by Robin Williams).

Try contrasting any of the following:

- The image from the background
- Your main colour and secondary colour
- Your clothing and your situation (like any fish-out-of-water film)
- Conceptual opposites (e.g. big and small, old and new, serious and silly)

Examples

Shappi Khorsandi's tour show poster uses contrast (specifically, conceptual opposites) not once but twice – in the name of the show and in the image. It's called *Skittish Warrior* and the poster has her dressed in armour but holding a cute bunny. Unsurprisingly, it's very effective.

An ad for *Austentatious, An Improvised Jane Austen Novel* recently cropped up on my feed, featuring the cast wearing period costumes but with modern day surroundings and objects. Another simple and strong contrast.

Little twists

Sometimes, you don't need to change everything. Just one small tweak is enough. Look at the different elements and think of how you could change them slightly to dramatise your show concept. This has been part of my approach to my own posters – they are all basically headshots on a plain background, I've just tweaked my head each time.

Sex and danger

You don't need to use these gratuitously, but if your show concept already has some visceral content then you don't need to be overly prudish either. There's no doubt that they can be effective elements. Many a classic

Head in jar for *When Magic & Science Collide*

Head as light bulb for *Oliver Meech's Improvised Magic Show*

magic poster (e.g. the bullet catch) shows some element of danger. And as some cabaret and burlesque posters have proved, you can be suggestive and still stay classy.

Minimalism

We'll cover this more in the Simple section, but think about how you could strip everything right back. I still remember the thrill of seeing the posters for Kill Bill, with their distinctive yellow background with the black strip. Not just the original poster, with Uma Thurman looking completely badass, but the complementary posters they ran at the same time, which had nothing but the yellow and black background. So minimalist, so recognisable, so iconic. Mwah!

Similarly, Alex Petty of Laughing Horse had some great posters made which were completely white with just a small line of text saying 'This poster intentionally left blank'. He made them just for fun (Alex rocks!) but interestingly, they were so eye-catching they would have made brilliant posters for an actual show.

This meets that

This is a classic approach to creating interesting visuals – combining one thing with another. In the case of most shows, you'll be looking to cross your face with the subject of your show. So, start by brainstorming all the objects or images that are associated with that subject, then see how you can apply them to your face.

Look beyond the bubble

In my early days of advertising, I attended a workshop by advertising legend Dave Trott. He drew a very simple diagram to illustrate a powerful point. He drew two long, thin ovals, one on each side of a flipchart page.

Then he added some dots inside each. Next, he drew some lines across, each connecting a dot on the left with the dot on the right. His point was that, if creativity is essentially joining the dots by connecting two ideas, then the more you can fill your brain with varied content, the more chances you give yourself to make interesting connections that lead to original ads.

An important part of that idea is the word 'varied'. It's easy to indulge exclusively in what you love, whether that's theatre, or comedy, or magic. The targeting of YouTube and social media doesn't help matters, as what you see actively becomes more focused and less diverse over time. But if you're doing a comedy show, and only ever consume comedy, then it's a lot harder to come up with something truly original. After all, you can't think outside the box if you never watch anything outside of it. So, fill your brain with anything and everything – browse bookshops, go to markets, flick through vinyl record sleeves, see shows and exhibitions that you wouldn't normally be drawn to. Note down interesting concepts and images whenever you see them.

Doctor Brown shook up stand up by bringing in neo-clowning influences. You can embrace outside influences to do the same thing with show posters.

A personal example

I created a show with the title *Live Brain Surgery*, which had the subline 'magic meets neuropsychology'. So I brainstormed all the objects and images that I could think of associated with brain surgery, including surgical scrubs, brains and scalpels.

Then, I took each one and thought about how I could

combine them with my head. I drew little sketches of each, about the size of a passport photo. I showed the few that had most potential to a photographer and tried a few different shots. These were the results:

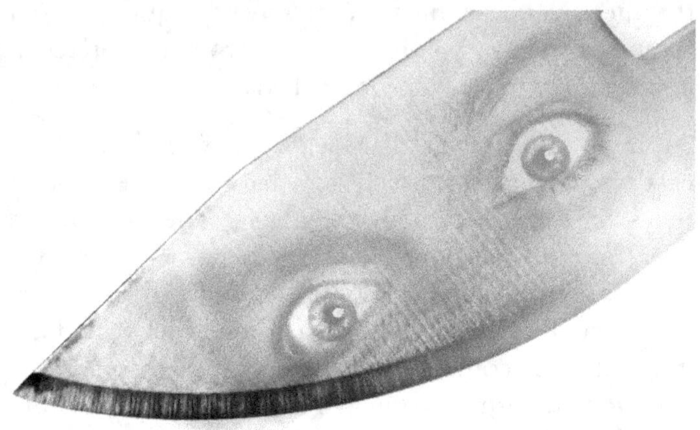

Eyes reflected in scalpel

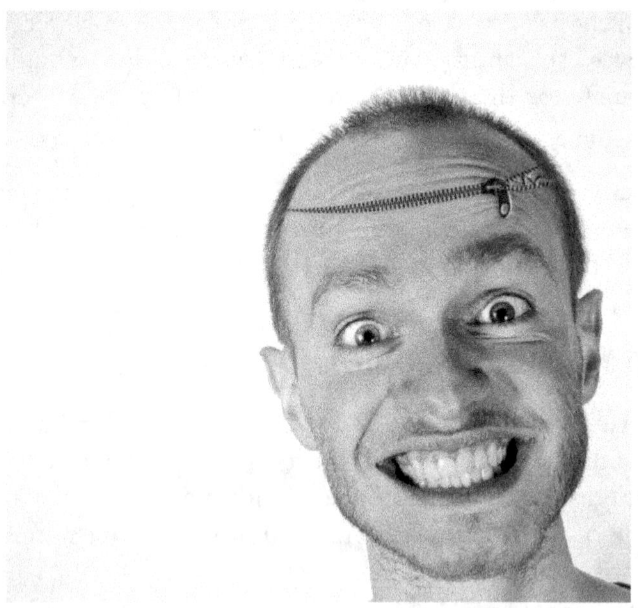

Head unzipped, with a manic smile

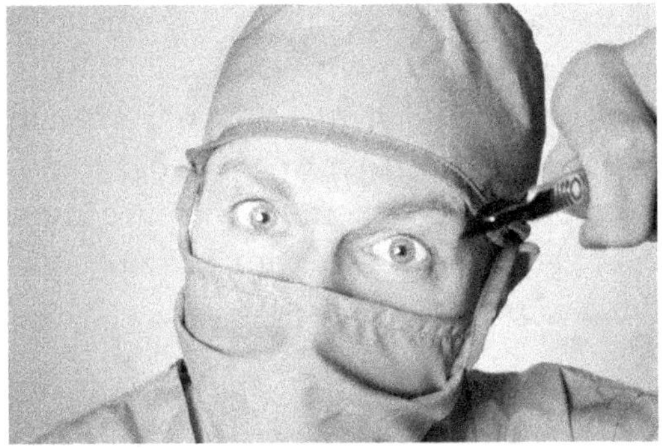

The unhinged surgeon look

They all sort of worked, but some suited the show better than others. The one with the eyes reflected in the scalpel was very eye-catching (as it were) but suggested a horror more than a comedy magic show. The same was true of me looking menacing in scrubs.

The head with the zipper also grabbed attention, but my expression was too maniacal. So I asked the photographer to do a version using my smiling face looking upwards, with just a hint of brain, and ended up with this:

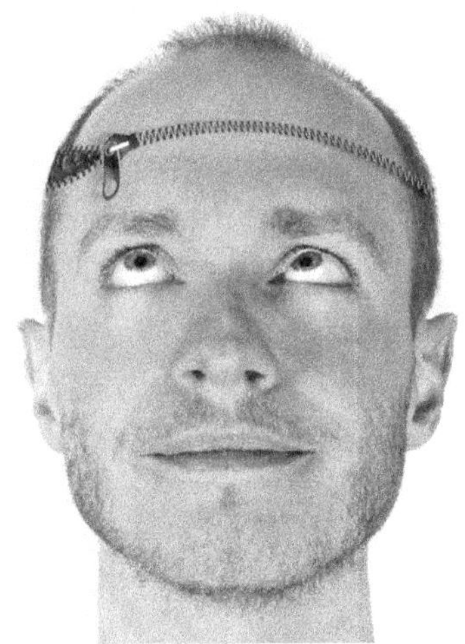

The final image for *Live Brain Surgery*

The result was a poster that I felt was dramatic enough to be remembered, but without being scary or off-putting. And happily, it worked. I had precious little marketing budget, was doing all my own flyering, and only had about 25 A3 posters up, yet many people came up to me and said 'oh, you're that guy with the zip'. And lots of people came to my show – a big relief.

I was also very pleased that I'd come to the photographer with an idea, rather than just seeing what happened on the shoot. He was a good photographer, but usually did fashion photography, so the scamp helped us to stay on the same page.

Try a similar process with your own show. List out what relates to your show, see how you can combine them with your head, make a shortlist, shoot them, and pick the one that works best.

If you don't have a particular subject, then go off your own personal style. And if you don't have anything else to go on, then pick a distinctive colour and go with that.

A classic example

The original Trainspotting posters are seen as classics. If you haven't seen them, give them a quick Google.

What makes them so striking?

They pick a really strong, distinctive colour scheme: bright orange with black and white photos of the stars.

Also, the characters have non-standard poses and expressions, avoiding the usual attractive-people-looking-glamorous approach.

As well as the main image-led poster, there was another

memorable text-led poster, which reprinted the iconic 'Choose Life' monologue. It's a testament to the impact that words can make. Given the thousands of shows in Edinburgh, I'm surprised that almost no-one has created their own tubthumping text-tastic poster. Maybe you can be the one.

Judgement day: selecting ideas

Now you have a bunch of ideas, it's time to don your judge's wig (metaphorically, though if you have one then by all means pop it on your pate). How do you select which ideas to pursue? Just use any of the following criteria.

What makes you excited?

Go with your gut. Sure, it may not be a highly rational approach, but then neither is being an artist! We work in such a subjective industry that trusting your creative instincts is as valid a way forward as any other.

What suits you?

Which feel like it fits your character or your show? If you're choosing between a few ideas, go for the one that you feel best represents your persona. If you're unsure, ask a friend for an outside perspective.

What's doable to a good standard, given your resources?

You don't want to be too boringly practical, as where there's a will, there's usually a way. That said, if an idea requires a cast of thousands, a tiger and bespoke facial prosthetics, and you've got 24 hours and a fiver to make it happen, then it's probably best to go with another idea.

What do you need, and what do you have?

This is related to the previous point. Think about what you need for each of the ideas, such as costumes, location, props, Photoshop skills, sets, props and backgrounds. Then rate each one in terms of what you have:

- Do you own it?
- If not, can you buy it without breaking the bank?
- If not, do you know someone who does?
- If not, it's worth a quick ask on social media, especially if it's something you'll just be borrowing for a shoot

Another way to think is the reverse: what do you already have access to that you can use? If you live in Brighton, can you use the seafront backdrop in a relevant way? If your friend has an adorable dog, can you borrow it for a shoot? Robert Rodriguez apparently used this approach with an early feature film, by creating a 'Rodriguez List' (mentioned in *Tools Of Titans* by Tim Ferris). Naturally, you want to keep it relevant to your concept, but it's easy to overlook what's right under your nose.

What feels fresh?

Sometimes, you'll come up with ideas that, while logically 'right', feel a bit obvious or familiar. In advertising, these are sometimes called 'first thoughts', since what springs to your mind first will likely spring to others' minds too. For this reason, go beyond first thoughts and you'll end up somewhere more interesting.

What feels scary?

If an idea is a bit different, or out there, and you're worried you might end up looking silly, it can be a good sign that you're on the right track to creating something really distinctive.

Pick a promising shortlist, not just The One

Just as show previews are important, because there's often a difference between what you think will work and what actually works, it's the same with ideas. Sometimes, a poster idea that's great in your head just doesn't 'pop' on paper. At the same time, your back-up ideas may turn out to be your favourite. Progressing a few options also stops you obsessing about perfection – since done is better than perfect (a phrase attributed to Sheryl Sandberg, amongst others). And having several images in the bag can be very handy when journalists want options, or if you need a few to swipe through on social media.

So, using the above criteria, circle a few favourites to do up. Now you're ready to make them a reality.

Get references, where appropriate

Draw small scamps of your shortlisted posters. While I generally recommend basing your poster on content over style, sometimes having a strong visual style can help an otherwise generic poster stand out. If you have a strong desire to use a particular style, that is hard to express in a black-and-white scamp (e.g. a poster that's designed exclusively in different shades of red), then find an example (e.g. a Rothko painting) that you can show alongside your scamp to help communicate your idea.

Ask around

You can always ask friends, family, or people on social media what they think. If you do, just bear three things in mind:

1. Offer them an A or B choice of two posters. If you just ask if they like one image, you won't get much helpful feedback.

2. Keep in mind that they are not necessarily your audience – if your show is aimed squarely at *Star Trek* fans (like me), then showing it to the general public and getting feedback that suggests removing 'that weird V-shaped hand sign' isn't very helpful.

3. Their taste may not match your taste. The people who like or dislike your design probably aren't designers, and their taste may be very different to yours. There are also some areas of life where the norms of design are quite different to others e.g. school newsletters' love of Comic Sans font.

Despite that cascade of caveats, if you show two posters and there's an overwhelming favourite, then it's probably worth listening to. It can also be useful for things you haven't spotted because you're too close to your own work. For example, I wrote a magic book for magicians called *The Plot Thickens*, and had the idea of doing a typographic cover, where the word thickens was so 'thick' that the 'T' and 's' were both slightly cropped by the edge of the cover. I thought it was a conceptually consistent minimalist mini-masterpiece. That was until a few people started asking me why I'd called my book *The Plot Chickens*.

The cover that fell foul (fowl?) of clarity.

I've heard that there's a similar two-point check that designers do with a new logo, which is:

Have I inadvertently designed something that looks like –

a.   A Nazi swastika

b.   A set of genitals

For that reason alone, I'd show your poster to at least one other person before printing 100 of them.

Stuck for ideas?

Don't worry if you're feeling stumped. We all hit a wall sometimes. Here's a few things that may help you get unstuck:

Embrace bad

If you're stalled because you're worried about creating a bad poster, the answer is to… create a bad poster. Actively tell yourself that you're going to make 10 bad posters and do that. Once the pressure's off, the ideas will come, and some may turn out not to be so bad after all.

Push on through for another 10 minutes

Sometimes just carrying on for a little longer can get you past an impasse. You don't have to go all punch-the-wall-macho and chain yourself to a desk for hours, often just a few more minutes can make all the difference.

Take a break

By contrast, sometimes when you feel creatively spent, it's best to step away for a bit. Get up, move around, make a cuppa, go to the loo, browse online (briefly). As with solving crossword clues, it's amazing how often relaxing your focus for a while leads to the answer popping into your head. I've lost count of the number of times a good idea has popped into my head during a tea break. (This use of the subconscious, for want of a better word, is mentioned in *A Technique For Producing Ideas* by James W. Young).

Go for a walk

For whatever reason, getting your body moving often gets your brain moving too.

Sleep on it

You may not awake in the night with a fully formed poster, but it'll give you a chance to come back to the challenge with a fresh mind. Giving ideas the 'overnight test' is also good for judging them objectively in the cold light of day, once the excitement of having the idea wears off.

Twist what you've got

It can be easy to get into a spiral of obsessively coming up with more and more new ideas, dismissing everything you've done before. If you find yourself doing this, it's worth looking back over your ideas. Often, you'll find something that's almost there, that just needs a small tweak to make it work. The zip-head poster for *Live Brain Surgery* is a good example of this. I could have seen that the initial image of the brain wasn't working and ditched the whole thing. But thankfully, keeping the idea and just tweaking the execution of it turned a not-quite-working poster into one of my favourites.

Don't overlook clear in your quest for genius

There's definitely a Goldilocks zone when creating ideas. You don't want to under-think things, but you don't want to over-think them either. If you've spent ages on your idea, and end up with something very lateral, or you've taken multiple creative leaps, then it's worth running it past someone for a fresh pair of eyes. That way, you can make sure you haven't ended up too far way, and that your poster still quickly communicates what your show is about. In the same way, don't be afraid to be obvious (as I learnt on an improv course run by The Spontaneity Shop).

Worth a thousand words

Hopefully you've now chosen an image, or a few images, that you're happy with. If you have, well done. If you haven't, don't fret, as the next section may help spark some more ideas. The best images, like the best posters, don't just communicate, they stand out. And that's our next step.

STAND OUT

What's one word that will never be pulled from a review to use on a performer's poster?

Offensive? Terrible?

No, it's 'generic'.

It's a term that rarely breeds success. Well, except maybe for boybands.

Check out this list:

Red, Orange, Yellow, Green, Blue, Indigo, Monkey.

At this point, you're probably thinking, what's with the monkey? It's a quick example of the power of standing out. And it works just as well for shows as for lists.

Often in life, the best way forward is to find someone who's doing something, and learn from the way they do things. It's a great strategy if you're learning to knit. But it's a terrible strategy for eye-catching posters.

Yet it's one that's easy to fall into. You want to get things right. So you look at a few posters for shows like yours.

You do something similar. Your poster logically expresses your show. Your poster looks a bit like theirs. You feel safety in numbers. Then you see it on a wall blending in with 50 other posters, and your heart sinks. You did everything logically right. But the result didn't stand out. And that's no fun. So, let's get lateral.

The first step is deciding to stand out. Since most people don't, you'll already be a step ahead. There are a few reasons why people don't stand out. Firstly, it's easier not too. When we think of a poster, our first thought is going to be the logical option. Fitting in also feels reassuring. Everyone else is doing it, so why shouldn't you? Also, if you don't stand out, then you can't be mocked it if doesn't work. It's like the classic, depressing business saying that nobody ever got fired for buying IBM. And nobody ever got mocked for producing a generic poster. But I'll bet nobody became a break-out hit from one either.

In this case, playing safe is actually pretty risky. After all, if your poster just gets lost among the others, then all the time and money you spent on it has been wasted.

Standing out means your show is more likely to be noticed and remembered. And that increases the chance of selling more tickets. It also means that each poster and flyer works harder, so you can spend less time flyering and more time relaxing (or stressing about other things!).

How to stand out

The main way to stand out is through your show title, and your show image. I'll focus mainly on the show image here, since most performers have often sorted and submitted their title before their image. That said, you can apply the same principles to make your show title stand out too.

Thankfully, by the time you've applied all the other aspects of STEPS, your poster will already stand out to some extent:

- Most posters are cluttered. Yours will be **simple**
- Most posters have too few or too many quotes. Yours will have a few short, **tempting** ones
- Most posters are vague. Yours will clearly **educate**
- Most posters are generic. Yours will be **personal**

The next step in standing out from the norm is pinning down exactly what the norm is. If you're able to go to a Fringe before you take a show there (the kind of admirable forward planning I never managed!), then snap some photos of a few walls with posters on. Both generally, and in the venue where you're thinking of performing. Also look though the programme, either printed or online.

Take five minutes to make a list of what the norms are in the promo materials.

While it varies a bit from year to year, there are some norms that seem to be consistently true.

The norms

For comedy shows, it will have a picture of the person holding a microphone.

For magicians, it's the following:

- Holding a fan of cards
- Holding a finger to their lips – supposedly charming, usually creepy
- Secretly palming a card
- Having a playing card tie

For show posters more generally, it's the following:

- Portrait
- A3
- Often a black background
- Lots of different fonts and colours
- Layouts that are either a bit scattershot or a bit square and blocky
- Font sizes that are either big and shouty, or small and hard to read
- Lots of film poster parodies

Now you know the norm, it's easier to stand out from it.

Techniques for standing out

Here are a few simple but powerful ways to stand out:

Do the opposite

Go through your list of norms, one at a time, and do the opposite. For example, instead of using a black background, make a light and airy poster with a white background. This sounds almost too simple, but it really works.

You don't need to do the opposite of every single norm, just choose one or two aspects and you'll stand out strongly.

Subvert the norm

You can still reference the norms, but actively separate yourself from them. This way, you can use the recognition shortcut of 'oh, it's a magic show' then add a 'but with a twist'. Barry & Stuart did this really well by taking the classic rabbit icon and making it look dark and twisted, which perfectly fits their style of subversive magic.

Question assumptions

The hardest thing about assumptions is that we often don't realise we're making them. At least, until someone else points them out, or does something to question them. But here's a really fun way to actively question them. Make a list of every assumption made about the poster, then question each one. Here are ten assumptions to get you going:

1. It has to feature a photo (as opposed to a graphic, animation, object, collage, etc.)
2. It has to be of me.
3. It has to show my whole face, facing forwards, looking towards the camera.
4. It has to be the right way up.
5. It has to be shot straight on, both horizontally and vertically.
6. It has to be in a well-lit studio with a plain background.
7. It has to have the name of the show above me.
8. It has to have writing on, that's upright and printed (not handwritten).
9. It has to work on a single poster, and all posters have to be the same.
10. It has to be a poster.

Every assumption you question could lead to a great poster. For proof, check out Chris Levine's portrait of Queen Elizabeth II. It takes someone who's featured in more portraits than you can shake a sceptre at, and makes us see her afresh, just by capturing her with her eyes closed. For another example, check out any of the posters for *The Play That Goes Wrong*. Each one twists a different assumption, including falling type, negative reviews, and upside-down posters.

Be random

The usual approach is to start with your show concept and think outwards from there. This makes logical sense, but that can also be the problem. If you go from A to B to C, you may end up at D or E, but you're unlikely to leap straight to Z.

This is where Random Word Stimulation can come in. I first came across this in *Lateral Thinking* by Edward De Bono. While it's not something I use all the time, it can be useful in freeing up your thinking, especially if your show topic is in a well-trodden area (e.g. stand-up comedy about relationships or Shakespeare plays).

The idea is simple: just look up a random word from the dictionary and use that to spark some creativity. Because our brains are good at making associations, there's a good chance that you will be able to find a connection, but the process will take you somewhere fresh.

For this reason, if the word you come across doesn't immediately seem related, try to resist the urge to keep grabbing at words until you find a 'good fit'. Because if you do that, then your Random Word Stimulation won't be particularly random, or stimulating.

As an example, say you're doing a new version of Romeo and Juliet. Over the centuries, most of the obvious associations have been done to death (as it were). So you look up a random word – clicking 'random article' on Wikipedia is good for this – and end up with: 'bite'. Now see what connections you can find between Romeo and Juliet and bite. Biting happens with the mouth, so show two mouths kissing, shot side on, so the two 'half' mouths make a whole mouth. Or maybe you go off famous biters, vampires, and create something with a *Twilight* feel. Or you cover the poster with big bold headlines with bite (as in attitude), like 'PUNCH-UPS, PASSION & POISON'. All valid options, and all different from where a logical approach would probably have taken you.

Be naughty, or wrong

Not in a way that would get you arrested, or put on a register. But 'breaking' the rules and norms is a good way of finding originality, precisely because most people mindlessly follow them.

Ask yourself, what kind of poster would you do if you were trying to get into trouble? In a rebellious way, not a criminal way – think Banksy more than bestiality (unless that's what your show's about).

Similarly, what would be completely the wrong way to do it? Could you miss off crucial pieces of information? Or actively make it difficult for people to come to your show?

Change your pose, or your expression

You don't need to change everything to stand out. At times, just changing your pose or your expression can be enough. Maybe you're the stand-up who always sits down. Or you're a slumpy, grumpy A Cappella singer. As with all these things, just decide what the norm is, then go another way.

Limit yourself

As we know from art, limitations can often open up creativity. The limit can be almost anything, including time (*Groundhog Day*), place (any bottle episode), number of takes (*Russian Ark*), budget (*The Blair Witch Project*), colour (*Sin City*), cast size (*One-Man Christmas Carol*) or senses (*A Quiet Place*).

In the same way, limiting yourself within a poster can make it more creative.

Try limiting the:

- Colour – use a single dominant colour
- Size – of yourself, or the poster itself
- Image – only show part of your face, or don't show yourself at all
- Production – don't print your posters the usual way
- Information – make your venue secret, or your show, or your name
- Number of posters – spend your entire budget producing one beautiful, framed poster. Perhaps have uniformed security guards to police it

Do more, or less

I'm always suspicious of people who claim there is only one way to do things, as you can almost always find an example of someone being just as successful taking the opposite approach. That's why there are two options for this tip, both of which can be effective.

Say you're doing a stand-up show about a shy coffee barista. Your starting point is a picture of you standing with a coffee cup. To make it more interesting, try doing more, and then doing less, to see if they take you somewhere interesting.

Do more: picture yourself half-hidden behind a wall of 100 disposable coffee cups (don't forget to recycle them afterwards).

Do less: picture one giant coffee cup filling the page, with the top of your head peeking above the cup's rim.

Additional approaches

For more strategies for creative thinking, I can recommend the book *Thinkertoys* by Michael Michalko, and the associated *Thinkpak* deck of prompt cards. Or, if it's still available, check out *Oblique Strategies*, based on Brian Eno's list of ways to create – available as a deck of cards and as a website.

If in doubt…

Just start by stripping your poster back so it's very simple and minimalist. As most posters are overly busy, this is often an easy, reliable way to make your poster stand out.

But what about those big stars who just have a poster of them wearing a suit? In the case of big-name stars with generic posters, the show is largely being sold on their name alone, so it doesn't need to be creative. That said, I personally think it's still a missed opportunity. Thankfully, it's not always the case. For instance, John Bishop has broad mainstream appeal in the UK, so could have gone for a standard poster without harming his ticket sales. Yet the poster for his *Winging It* tour still has him sitting on the wing of a plane, rather than in a standard studio.

One caveat: stand out but make sense

Sometimes people think that standing out at all costs is a good thing. Unfortunately, this tends to lead to 'gratuitous creativity', for want of a better phrase. It's like the old poster that says 'SEX! Now I've got your attention, come to my economics lecture.' It may grab people's attention, but it doesn't reward their attention.

There's a classic acronym in direct marketing known as AIDA. It stands for Attention, Interest, Desire and Action – the four stages your writing should take the audience through. If we don't grab people's attention with something that's linked to our show, they won't progress past Attention to Interest, Desire and then the Action of buying a ticket. The best way to stay on track is to focus on dramatising the show's concept in an interesting way.

But what if there's nothing interesting about my show, I hear our neurotic-performer-brain cry? Relax – every show has something interesting about it. If it didn't, you wouldn't be doing it! So, if in doubt, start with what attracted you to your show.

Another caveat: you don't have to be extreme to stand out

Stuart Goldsmith, seasoned stand-up and host of the endlessly engrossing *The Comedian's Comedian* podcast, had a poster for his show *An Hour* that stood out, without being extreme. It was down to the style of the photography. The picture featured him wearing a jumper, shot outdoors, in natural light, in a warm, human, un-glossy way. It was a beautiful, honest photo – the opposite of the slick, soulless studio shots many others produce. In doing so, he stood out while staying true to his performing style.

For my last few posters, I made them stand out by warping my face in some way, using Photoshop. But I kept it relevant by warping my face in a way that suited the show's theme:

- For *Live Brain Surgery*, which was all about the brain, I added a zip across my forehead, partially unzipped to expose my brain beneath

- For *When Magic & Science Collide*, about science and sci-fi, I put my head in a jar

- For *Oliver Meech's Improvised Magic Show*, about having ideas for tricks on the fly, I turned my head into a lightbulb

- For *When Magic & Food Collide*, I impaled my head on a fork

The concepts may sound extreme, but I took care that the final versions were not. Why? Because I've been told by audiences that I come across as warm and approachable, and wanted to convey that, so I was careful to avoid anything too gruesome. You can apply a similar approach to your own posters – to paraphrase the old saying, it *is* what you do, *and* the way that you do it. Find a concept to communicate your show, and then adjust the tone to suit your style.

Stand out and deliver

Now you have the makings of a poster that outshines other shows and commands attention. Next, you want to turn that attention into a desire to see your show. How? By making it more tempting.

TEMPTING

This section deals with our second audience question – Is it any good? In other words, is it tempting?

This links to one of the many myths surrounding Fringe festivals, which is that people are seeing lots of shows so they'll take a punt on a random one.

Actually, most people are only there for a few days so they may only be seeing around 10 shows, and the cost of paid shows can quickly add up, so their time and money is actually pretty scarce.

So, when you come to answering question two later on, don't think of it as selling, but as reassuring.

The more investment you're asking people to make, the more reassurance you need to give them. And that investment can be money, time, commitment, risk, etc.

At one end of the spectrum, if you're offering a free mixed-bill comedy show in the venue your audience are already drinking in, starting in five minutes, then you're asking for a low investment, so you don't need to offer much reassurance.

At the other end, if it's a show featuring a single performer, with a high ticket price, in a venue far from others, which lasts over an hour, then you need a lot more reassurance.

Matching your level of reassurance to the level of audience investment you require is one of the keys to selling your show well.

Here are a range of ways to make your show as tempting, and reassuring, as possible:

Stars

The strength of star ratings comes from their simplicity. They may not be highly informative, but they're a helpful visual-shorthand for 'this show is good'. So, if you have any four or five star reviews, then feature them proudly. This is also one place where repetition isn't redundant. The more the merrier – if you're lucky enough to have loads then by all means stick them on your poster, just order or group them in a way that can be quickly digested by busy punters.

Press quotes from reviews

For all we like to moan about reviews, they are still annoyingly useful for selling your show. Like stars, they reassure people that the show's worth seeing. But unlike stars, they also give punters a feel for your show. So, scour your reviews for positive comments you can use. Or, if you prefer not to read them for your mental health, then get someone you trust to read them and pull out the juicy bits on your behalf.

When using reviews, it's worth considering two things: the length and the source.

Length

The need for brevity applies to review quotes (a.k.a. pull quotes) just as much as your own words. Generally, the shorter the pull quote, the better – especially on your poster. If you have the luxury of choosing between two similar quotes, I'd choose the shorter one every time. And, without changing their meaning, find the shortest section of the quote that you can use. Adjectives are you friends here. If the quote is: "This show was simply astounding", just use the word "astounding". Some may argue you lose some of the nuance, but it's worth it for the increased speed of comprehension. Just think, you could feature five single-word-superlative quotes for the same word-count as that one longer quote.

If you really can't trim it to the bone, and sometimes you'll have a lovely review that's frustratingly unshrinkable, then highlight the key words in the quote (making them bigger or bolder) to help people focus on them first. We'd love to believe that punters pour over our posters, but in reality most will just give them a speedy skim.

Source

Not all reviewers are created equal. Rightly or wrongly, most punters will give a national newspaper or TV show more weight than a student blog. So who the quote is from is as important as the quote itself. Make their relative prominence reflect their importance. You can do this either by having your more prestigious reviews higher up on the poster, so they're seen first. Alternatively, make less impressive publications smaller in size.

You can see a similar thing in action on book covers. With

newer authors, the book title will often be larger than their name. While with bestselling authors like Steven King, or Sophie Kinsella, their names will dominate. Obviously, as with everything, use your judgement. Don't use several different font sizes for the publications on your poster. That would look messy. Instead, take a collective view on how impressive your publications are and size them accordingly.

Celebrity endorsement

Much as I find society's obsession with 'slebs' a bit depressing, there's no doubt that many people value their opinion. So if you have a nice quote from someone famous, then use it. They don't necessarily need to be super famous either. There are many people who are well-known within their particular niche (e.g. magic, science, *Doctor Who*), even if they're not household names. If you're doing a show based around that particular niche, then aiming to get a nice comment from them can pay off.

Brands

People trust certain brands. And brands come in all shapes and sizes. Google and Coke are brands, but so are the BBC and the National Theatre. So again, if you have a connection to a brand, use it. Similarly, I once travelled hundreds of miles to do a radio interview, so I could add their brand name to the places where I'd appeared. And I know from talking to audience members that it helped convince them to come. Think creatively (but honestly!) about how you can add some respected brands to your performing biog.

TV or YouTube

Telly sells tickets. It's been that way for decades. And

it's why comics clamour to get on panel shows, even if they find them emotionally challenging and creatively uninspiring. Of course, it's not easy to get on TV, but there are ways if you really want to. At the time of writing, there's *Britain's Got Talent*, if you want to go that route. There are also many more channels these days to approach. There may be sideways approaches too, by using any interesting skill you may have to appear on an existing, unrelated programme. For example, the quiz contestant who can also beatbox, or the aspiring dancer who can also do magic.

Alternatively, start putting out content on YouTube (or Instagram, or any other online platform) and then quote your views or followers on your poster. If you get a big enough following, you could even skip the poster all together, and sell out your run before you arrive. I wouldn't rely on that, but it's a nice possibility to consider.

Social proof

Essentially, this approach is 'if other people like it, it must be good'. In practice, this means using comments and tweets as quotes. Thankfully, in these days of social media dominance, people are more used to seeing reviews from people who aren't reviewers. You'll even see it on boards outside West End shows.

Make the unfamiliar familiar

Taking a leap in the dark can be scary for people. Thankfully, everything's like something, and that goes for shows too. As mentioned in the Educational section, if you can suggest that your show is like another show, or a combination of shows, then it helps punters feel like they're taking less of a giant leap and more of a small step.

Modesty is overrated

Years back, when I was applying to university, I wrote a draft of my Personal Statement which was sprinkled with jokey jibes at my own abilities. I remember showing it to my big sister and she said, "Now is not the time for self-deprecation". I bristled, but she was right. Sure, self-deprecation can sometimes be charming, even if I'm not that great at it (boom boom). But, with a few exceptions, preparing your poster is not one of those times. Nor is it the time to be overly modest – something that seems to be especially hard to fight if, like me, you're British.

I remember feeling like I should take my Fringe sell-out show laurels and tuck them tastefully away at the edges of my poster. Then I walked past a poster for *Hot Dub Time Machine* which had a big bold banner right across it declaring TWO SELL-OUT RUNS, or words to that effect. It should be obvious, but the old showbiz saying remains true: if you've got it, flaunt it. Make the most of your assets. You don't have to be crass, but at the same time, don't hide your light under a bushel.

Sell-out shows and runs

Street performers will tell you that a crowd draws a crowd. For that reason, I have a personal theory that a sell-out show is a bigger draw than a 5-star show, perhaps because it hints at demand outstripping supply. If you've had a sell-out performance, or run, then mention that. If it happened at another festival then mention that. And remember that when punters see a sell-out show, they don't usually ask, "Yes, but how big was the venue?". Ethically, I wouldn't take this to ridiculous extremes, but you don't have to be filling arenas to be a 'sell-out' – filling a 40-seat venue for a month is still an achievement, especially at festivals when the average audience is apparently around four people.

Make it easy

People are lazy. Not everyone, obviously, but from the invention of the dishwasher and the washing machine, to the proliferation of the word 'effortless' in ads for tech products, a good rule of thumb is that most people will mostly choose to do things the easy way. So make it simple to get to your venue, or at least seem that way. Make the venue name clear (and the venue number if there is one). Flyer close to your venue, offer a map, mention that it's "just 3 minutes away", "just down the road" or "just next door". Make your entertainment effortless to enter.

Make it good value, if it is

If it's a good deal, say so. Just The Tonic even call their comedy show *The Big Value Comedy Show*. How is your show good value? Can you add a family ticket? If there's a big cast, or a live band, or a free croissant, mention it on your poster. We'd love to think that people come to shows purely for our artistic vision, but people love a good deal, even when they're seeing a show. It's maybe not worth warping your show vision for, but if you happen to be giving people more bang for their buck then make sure you let them know about it.

The other side of temptation

As well as making your show more tempting, you can also make it less un-tempting. In other words, you want to remove any 'barriers to purchase', as they're known, by addressing anything that might stop people buying a ticket.

Here are six potential barriers to purchase, and how you can overcome them:

1. Too expensive: include 2 for 1 offers, previews, and weekday rates. Or give justifications for the price in your poster (e.g. if it's a highly exclusive limited run, or it's in a lavish venue).

2. Not free: make it free, or join the growing group of Pay What You Want shows.

3. Might not be good: reduce the perceived risk with positive reviews of your show, or if you don't have any yet, of your previous shows.

4. Too far away: show a map, mention its proximity to a well-known landmark, or flyer nearer to the venue. I chose to flyer at a particular spot so I could tell people my show was "just 2 minutes down there".

5. Too niche: suggest that it's really for everyone. You can either directly state this yourself, or, even better, do so through a review. For example, *'You'll love it, even if you think you don't like juggling'* (or 'opera', or 'burlesque', or any other less-mainstream genre). You can also broaden the show's scope through the themes. Take *Billy Elliot*. Most people can't immediately relate to being a Northern male child ballet dancer, but they can relate to being an outsider, overcoming doubters and chasing their dream.

6. Needs pre-existing knowledge: I addressed this in the blurb for *When Magic & Science Collide*. To avoid people worrying that they might need to know a lot about science, I added this: 'No knowledge of science required. Just a mind that's open and a jaw that's ready to drop.'

These reassurances are partly there for the main person who's tempted by your show, but mainly there for their 'plus 1'. In any group, there will normally be someone who proposes the show, who then tries to convince their friend/partner/spouse/lover/butler to come too. It's the same reason that some Indian restaurants have a nominal omelette on the menu – not for the curry-lovers, but for their spice-spurning partners.

I've had a barrier with my own shows, where some people read 'family-friendly' and assume it's a 'kids show'. Actually, it's for everyone – the usual adult fringe crowd plus all the families too. Like Freddie Mercury, I want it all. So I've used 'Ages 7-107' to remove the barrier. I've seen other performers (e.g. the enviably energetic Javier Jarquin, Card Ninja) use PG film ratings for a similar reason.

For completeness, here are two other classic psychological techniques which you could also try –

- Scarcity: 'For one night only', 'Only UK shows', 'A rare chance', "Can someone get me a ticket?" (a quote used to advertise *The Book of Mormon* musical)
- FOMO (Fear Of Missing Out): Don't miss…

Just use these with caution, so you don't end up sounding like a creepy mind meddler!

Making a tempting proposition

By using a combination of blurb, reviews, quotes, tweets and helpful clarifications, you have made your show as tempting as possible, by giving them lots to like, and little to not-like.

Next up, you'll learn how to give them something even more important – you.

PERSONAL

The simplest performing advice is also the trickiest.

Be yourself.

It's the kind of glib tip which is easy to say but nearly impossible to apply, because we're all a bit too close to ourselves.

But it's what your audience wants. They want you. It's what will make your show unique, and your poster unique. So how do you make your poster more personal? There's the rub.

If you're one of those lucky people who knows exactly who they are from an early age (while the rest of us are still flailing and failing) then just express that.

If you're not sure, then read on.

The essentials

First off, include your name prominently in your show title and poster. This should be obvious, but I got so enamoured with my clever-clever (but not smart) title for my first show, *Time Warper*, that I made it really big on my poster, and made my name tastefully small (actually, barely legible).

My first show poster

Similarly, I didn't include a picture of my face. These were both missed opportunities.

Since your show name and image are about the only guaranteed chances for publicity you can get, make sure you feature both. I'd realised my mistake by the following year, and had both my name and my face prominently featured.

Extra credit

Your name and your face are enough for a good, personal poster. But there are ways to take it up a notch, if you wish. That said, it's easy to become overwhelmed when creating a poster, so treat the rest of this chapter as optional extras you can consider adding if you wish.

Defining your brand

Thinking about 'your personal brand' is enough to make any self-respecting artist be a little sick in their mouth. So instead, just think of it as what makes you, you. Or at least the onstage version of you.

Here are eight ways to do that:

1. Ask people who know you well

Start with your family and friends: ask them to sum you up in three words. Do this a bunch of times and then see if any particular adjectives keep cropping up. This is a good guide to how you are perceived.

2. Read your reviews

Yes, I know reviews can be a gateway to self-flagellation and despair, but if you can get through that, reviewers are used to quickly summing up performers, so they may throw out useful hints about how you come across. If you're sticking to a no-review diet, then as a workaround, ask a friend to read them for you, and pull out any positive adjectives and snippets you could use.

3. Complete a quiz

As a young teenager in the nineties, I used to sneak a peek at my sister's girls' magazines. As well as being the closest thing to sex education that most British kids got back then, they were always good for a personality quiz. So here's a similar quiz I've created, but for defining your onstage persona rather than anything steamier or unseemlier.

Grab a pen and paper, go down this list, and quickly pick one of each option:

- Loud or quiet
- High, medium or low energy
- High, medium or low status
- Warm or cold
- Playful or serious
- Masculine or feminine
- Logical or lateral
- Engaged or detached
- Real or fantastical
- Adult or family-friendly
- Insider or outsider
- Cool or cheesy
- Classical or contemporary
- Thoughtful or emotional

In terms of my onstage persona, I'm loud, high energy, medium status, warm, playful, feminine (or at least non-macho), lateral, engaged, fantastical, family-friendly, outsider, cheesy, contemporary and thoughtful.

What's your persona? Once you know, you'll have a clearer sense of how to express that in your poster.

If you're warm, use warm colours.

If you're loud, use bold fonts.

If you're classical, use classical serif fonts.

You get the idea.

4. The wine tasting approach

No, I'm not suggesting you can find your true self by getting sozzled (though some may disagree). This is the idea that if you are challenged to describe a wine by itself, it can be tricky. Yet take sips of two different wines, and it's suddenly a lot easier to compare and contrast. So, if you found the quiz tricky, then pick another performer, and consider the ways that you differ from them.

For example, comparing myself to Jack Dee:

He's grumpy, low energy and detached (and brilliant at playing that persona).

I'm upbeat, high energy and engaged.

Try the same thing with yourself.

5. You are what you like

This isn't always the case, but sometimes it can be helpful. For example, I love Eddie Izzard, *Back To The Future*, and eye-catching adverts. They are playful, upbeat, idea-packed escapism. Same goes for my shows.

Knowing that, you can make your poster accordingly.

6. You in one word

How would you sum yourself up in a word? There are plenty of well-known comedians you can do it with (e.g. Freewheeling = Ross Noble, Surreal = Noel Fielding, etc.). If you're not sure, ask people who've seen you perform, or if your ego can take it, ask online. Don't obsess over any particular word, but if the same one keeps cropping up then it's worth noting.

Also, be aware that this can evolve as you grow as an artist. Early in my career I was described in a couple of reviews as "endearing". It's not a bad word, but it's a bit more low-status than I'd have liked. A few years later, when I'd racked up more stage time, I found the word stopped appearing, as my increase in confidence must have started to come across on stage. So keep checking at occasional intervals that your poster stays in line with people's current perception of you.

7. Pick an emotion

Do you favour a particular emotion or state in your shows? For mine, it's probably enthusiasm. What's yours? Anger, melancholy, joy, bitterness, mania? If you have one, you can use it to influence your poster. If you're light and bright onstage, you're unlikely to have a moody, monochrome poster, and vice versa (unless you're deliberately going for contrast). Look at album covers for good examples of people dramatising their music's emotions. For example, compare Iron Maiden and Katy Perry. Just don't do it right before bed or your dreams may be terrifying rather than teenage.

8. Listen to audiences

Paul Daniels said that he'd sometimes hide in the toilets after his shows, so he could hear how people described his show. These days, you can also get a feel by the words that people use when they mention your show on social media. For example, I tend to get the phrase 'great fun', so I try and convey that sense of fun in my posters.

One caveat

Just make sure there's not a disconnect between how you think you come across, and how you actually come across.

Since I was quite geeky at school, I tried out a joke in my shows about people looking at me and thinking "Didn't I used to bully you?". It didn't get a laugh, and after discussing it with someone later, I realised that it was because I no longer came across like a geeky teenager. Similarly, I love a bit of dark humour, but it never works for me on stage, as it doesn't gel with the nice-guy persona that I apparently give off. So I now know to avoid anything too dark or low status in my shows and posters.

It'll come

Luckily, with enough stage time, most performers develop a feel for what kind of character they are anyway.

Making it your own

Looking for more ways to be more distinct? Coming right up! You don't need to do all eleven of them, even one or two is enough to make your character clearer.

1. Find a hook

Developing an intriguing encapsulation of your act helps you to stick in their mind.

A good example of this is Chris Cox, who is 'The mind-reader who doesn't read minds'. It's paradoxical, which is intriguing, and sums up his playful approach to mind-reading.

Hooks, or labels, not only help people remember you, but journalists love them. Some examples:

- Derren Brown: Psychological Illusionist
- Madonna: The Material Girl
- Bruce Springsteen: The Boss
- Jamie Oliver: The Naked Chef

As ever, I'd recommend you come up with lots of options then pick (or get others to pick) some favourites. You can then use the top one (or top few) on a flyer and see which catch on.

In the same way that you can describe your show in terms of existing shows, you can also describe yourself in terms of other performers. If may feel like an affront to your individuality, but it's a quick way for people to 'get' you.

For instance, the inimitable Piff The Magic Dragon, was once described as "Jack Dee in a dragon costume". While Piff is so much more than that, it was a useful hook in the early days for British people to quickly get the gist of his character.

2. Get a gimmick

As the saying goes, you've gotta have a gimmick. Well, you don't have to, but it's something to consider. Here are a few different types that you may wish to adopt, along with relevant examples of stars, past and present.

Using your existing features:

Chris Evans: glasses and ginger hair (originally, anyway).

Adding something to your appearance:

Elton John: flashy glasses and jackets.

Russell Brand and Amy Winehouse: big hair (my lack of a more specific term for this tells you all you need to know about my knowledge of hairdressing).

Part time (i.e. you can take them off):

Jacqueline Wilson: big finger rings.

Daft Punk: robot helmets.

Tape Face: black eye shadow and tape over mouth.

Full time (i.e. they're permanent or hard to remove):

Angelina Jolie: tattoos.

Goldie: gold teeth.

Personally, I'm not an always-on performer, so I'd favour something part-time, but if you want to live the dream 24/7, then go for it.

On the other hand, don't worry if you don't have any of this. If you've got a face and name, that'll do fine. And even if you don't, then The Person With No Face Or Name sounds like a fringe show (or a Coen Brothers' movie).

3. Remember my name, fame

It can help if you have an unusual, memorable name. But it's not essential. For every Arnold Schwarzenegger, there's a Will Smith. For every Benedict Cumberbatch, there's a Martin Freeman.

4. Use a consistent colour

Noel Britten's *Bizarre Bath* tour is a long-running comedy walking tour. His branding and props are consistently purple. As well as making the show feel more internally consistent, it also helps make his branding instantly recognisable, especially for punters who are only visiting the city for a day or two.

5. Develop a logo

There's a reason all big companies have logos. They work. But why let corporations have all the fun? You can enjoy the benefits of a logo too, without having to wear a tie and use terms like 'thought leader'. I once heard logos described as like a bank account of goodwill (this analogy doesn't originate with me – if you know the reference, do let me know). Every time you put on a good show, it's like putting a deposit into your account. Then, when you have a new show, you can use the logo to cash in some of that goodwill, as people will bring those good associations to your new project. Frisky & Mannish have a logo, as does Dynamo , and it hasn't done their careers any harm! Why not do the same? Give some starting thoughts to a designer and have them come up with a few for you to choose from. Logos are also handy if you want to enter the wonderful make-more-money-so-I-can-actually-afford-to-live world of merch.

6. Use, and reuse, a pet word

Tim Key has used 'slut' in multiple show titles. After performing *When Magic & Science Collide*, I called a subsequent show *When Magic & Food Collide*. It can give the feeling of sequels, and gives a hint of 'if you liked this, then you'll like that'. That said, if your name is on every show, then that gives some consistency anyway, so don't worry too much about having a pet word.

7. Adopt a distinctive tone of voice

Russell Brand has a very distinctive style of language that is instantly recognisable. Is there a similarly distinctive tone that you can adopt? For instance, if most comedians have a low-status tone of voice, can you go deliberately high-status? For example, Tom Stade called one of his shows *You're welcome.*

8. Pick a font

Your fonts should suit you. This is a subject where it's definitely worth speaking to a designer. There are a few standard fonts that will work for most things. If you're going for an unusual one, get advice from a designer.

9. Have a unique silhouette

Matt Groening said that when designing *The Simpsons*, he made sure that the main characters had a unique silhouette. In a Russell Brand documentary (yes, him again), he said he was inspired by this to give himself big hair in an effort to achieve the same thing. How can *you* cut a fine figure?

10. Catchphrases

Don't force this, as there's nothing more naff than trying to force a catchphrase that isn't catchy (other than perhaps still using the word 'naff'). But if a phrase does crop up that you notice yourself, or others, repeating, then make the most of it.

11. Gestures

These can be separate, or combined with a catchphrase. The arm poses of Usain Bolt and Mo Farah are examples of the former. *Strictly Come Dancing's* "Keep dancing!" while rocking forwards in-hold is an example of the latter.

By the way, if the idea of gestures and catchphrases seems a bit cheesy, they needn't be. John Robertson's intense live gaming show *The Dark Room* includes the phrase: "YOU DIE! YOU DIE! YOU DIE!", which is definitely memorable and not cheesy in the least. Also, you can always deliver your catchphrases slightly ironically (e.g. Andy Zaltzman's "In the bin" at *The Bugle* podcast's live shows). That way, you can lose the cringe but keep the catchiness.

The ultimate test

If you covered up your name and pixelated your face, could people still tell the poster was for you? It's rare that people reach that truly iconic level, but it's a good goal to aim for.

Make yourself easy to remember, and to Google

Oliver is a common name. Meech is not. I always need to spell it out on the phone. What to do? If you're in a similar boat, you can either change your name to make it easier to remember (e.g. mind-reader Colin McCleod becoming Colin Cloud), or do the following:

Help them remember with mnemonics

Anything that helps them remember can work, from rhymes to twisting of existing phrases. A few examples:

- Comedian Joe Lycett inserted his name into a well-known song, for his show *Joe Lycett: That's The Way A-Ha A-Ha, Joe Lycett*

- Ventriloquist Jeff Dunham created a whole comedy routine based around his URL, to drum it into people's minds
- If you have a name that people consistently misspell the same way, you could get that as a second URL so you can redirect them to your main website
- Comedian Hari Kondabolu has a cunning approach to this (heard on *The Bugle*) where he tells people to just Google whatever way they think his name is spelt and let the search engine point them in the right direction

If you find something that works, don't be afraid to stick to it

Sometimes as artists, we get Shiny Object Syndrome, constantly craving newness. While it can lead to wonderful creativity, it's also okay to stay with what works. For me, warping my face on my posters was successful, so I've done that for a few shows. Carl Donnelly made *Now That's What I Carl Donnelly! Volume V*, followed by *Vol. VI*. Mining the same seam doesn't mean you can't mix things up if you want to, but it can help you to sort your posters quickly. That, in turn, frees up more time to focus on all the other aspects of your show which need attention.

You did it

Now you've added a personal touch to your poster, all the main elements are in place. The end is in sight! To finish off, we're going to switch from adding to subtracting — it's time to simplify.

SIMPLE

Keeping your poster simple should be simple, at least in theory. When you see a really simple advert, like a poster for an iPhone, it looks like there's not much to it. It seems like anyone could do it.

And making your poster simple *is* simple. You just say less, and show less. But that doesn't mean it's easy. Something similar is often said on running blogs about completing a marathon. It's simple – you just start running, then stop after 26.2 miles. But ask anyone who's actually done one (not me!) and they'll tell you that it's no walk in the park (or run on the road).

Take a look at any poster-plastered wall at a Fringe festival, and you'll see that in practice, making things simple can prove a challenge.

So, why bother?

Good question. Especially if you've designed your show to have depth, breadth, intelligence and complexity. Why dumb it down? Why patronise your audience? After all, people aren't stupid.

No, they're not. But they are busy, tired, and distracted.

When you start designing your show poster, it's natural to devote all your time and attention to it. And you should. You know your show inside out. And if you could guarantee that your poster would be seen by people who had plenty of time, were well rested, and could give it their full attention, that would be fine.

But the reality is the opposite. They're rushing from show to show. They haven't slept well because of partying / flatmates partying / late shows / early shows / indigestion / replacing a broken prop at 1am (hello fellow magicians). And they're overwhelmed by posters for hundreds of other shows.

It means that you're getting just a fraction of a fraction of their attention.

It's the same with flyers. Next time you're at a Fringe festival thoroughfare, take a moment to observe how long the average person looks at each flyer they are handed before either losing interest or being handed another flyer. Chances are it'll be about three or four seconds. The same goes for a poster. Imagine it's going by on a bus (in the case of some big names, it will be).

So, how do you overcome such tricky conditions? By keeping it simple.

I personally dislike the classic KISS acronym – Keep It Simple, Stupid. I prefer the nicer, if cheesier: Keep It Simple, Smarty. Because making your poster simple to understand is one of the smartest decisions you can make. It's also one of the best ways to make your poster stand out from all the other shows clamouring for attention on cluttered walls.

How to make your poster simple, or simpler

There are two steps:

1. Simplify your message.
2. Simplify your execution.

(N.B. By execution, I mean the way you present your message, rather than cold-blooded murder. Although the latter would certainly generate some publicity. Not that I'm recommending killing anyone. Okay, I'll stop digging. Not that I have anything to bury…)

Let's take them in turn.

1. Simplify your message

First off, answer the following questions:

What is the concept of your show?

How would you sum up your show in a sentence, of around 10 words?

If you're lucky, or savvy, your show will have a clear, simple concept, summed up in a clear, simple title. That way you won't have to add any other elements to explain it.

If you fall into that category, then congratulations – permission to feel briefly smug and treat yourself to a biscuit (just the one, mind – what are you, made of money?!).

If, like most of us, you're not so lucky or savvy, then read on (and come back to simplicity of concept when you start creating your next show).

If your show title happens to be a bit less explanatory, then I'd recommend adding a subtitle, which gives more of a feel for the show – either the premise or the tone.

Returning to our Hollywood poster analogy, this is the equivalent of your tagline:

e.g. *Alien* – 'In space, no one can hear you scream.'

House Of Wax (remake) – 'Prey. Slay. Display.' (one of my favourite taglines ever)

And, on the slightly less sophisticated side:
American Pie: The reunion – 'Jim's finally taking her up the aisle.'

A personal example

My first show struggled with simplicity. It was a one-man time-travelling magic show (different to the devilishly clever Morgan and West's time-travelling magic show, which debuted at the same festival). Coincidence? Or time travel?! (Coincidence).

Since I'm fond of wordplay, I called my show: *Time Warper*. I thought it was very clever. Other people, well, they weren't sure what to think. A one-man Rocky Horror tribute show, perhaps? Cue a rapidly added subline: 'Magic meets time travel'. True, it wasn't as creative, but it was much clearer. And more clarity equals more bums on seats. By the way, Morgan and West went with a more direct title: *'Morgan & West: Time-Travelling Magicians'*. Told you they were devilishly clever.

As a professional advertising creative, I should have slapped myself for making the mistake. But I didn't. Partly because I'm a lover, not a fighter. But mainly because it just goes to show that sometimes you are too close to your own show to see the woods for the trees. At least until something, or someone, encourages you to reassess things.

Another way to simplify

Try to eliminate elements, and prioritise the one or two things that you want to communicate above all else.

For instance, a fuller description of my show is that it's a family-friendly, one-person, time-travel-themed, interactive, comedy, stage magic show. Phew!

Way too much information. Keep It Simple, Smarty.

What are the one or two things that are most Tempting, or most unique (to make it Stand out)?

There are loads of stage, comedy and one-person shows. And quite a few interactive and family-friendly shows. But if I choose the magic and time-travel aspects, especially in combination, there are unlikely to be many other shows that are like it. (Or in my case, only one).

Another way to simplify is to complete this sentence:

It's a [adjective][type of show] about [concept].

e.g. It's a dark musical about a killer duck.

Perhaps it's called: *Who's quackers now?*

(Or *Kill Bill*, or *Ducktor Strangeglove*, or *Bread and buried*, or *Mallardjusted*, or… but I digress).

Simplifying? It's elementary

Now you have your title, and possible subtitle, add all the

other elements you think you need to your poster sketch. In advertising, these are often known as 'mandatories'.

Now, imagine that you're Bond or Nikita, and ruthlessly eliminate any element that isn't absolutely necessary. What's necessary? Ultimately, only you can decide, but here's a rough guide:

Elements you almost definitely need:

- Show title
- Your name
- Venue
- Starting time

Elements you may need:

- Logos for the fringe and the venue – though double-check if they're contractually essential or just would-be-nice. If you can end up with one logo rather than three then all the better.

Elements you might think you need but probably don't:

- Your Twitter, YouTube and other addresses: how often have you stopped and typed in one from a poster? Exactly. The only exception is if you have a compelling reason for people to watch something. In which case, it's still probably better on a flyer, since they can take it with them to watch later.
- Your website: again, would you check it out?
- QR codes: ugly, and commit the cardinal sin of advertising – they assume people care.
- Maps: probably save them for the flyer.
- Box office telephone: most people book online.
- Ticket prices: if they are a selling point, or they're

free, then maybe. If they're neither then I'd be tempted to leave them off.

It's not that any these things are inherently wrong, it's just that any potential benefit you gain from adding the information is offset by how they dilute your audience's attention.

So, after all that, what's left? The things you absolutely can't do without.

Now for a second opinion, show it to a friend and ask them if there's anything else that's superfluous? To borrow a phrase from my Mum, they're not 'ego-involved', so they may spot another element that you can do without.

Congratulations, you're now left with just the essentials, so you're already nearer to a great poster.

2. Simplify your execution

What you can't eliminate, minimise.

Take each element in turn and see if you can make it shorter or smaller.

Shorter

When I started out as a copywriter, I read advice that you should treat words as if they each cost you five pounds (adjust accordingly for inflation). Every word is valuable, so make each one count. If in doubt, cross out one word at a time and if it still makes sense without it, leave it out. Keep cutting it down until it stops making sense, then add back in the last word.

For example, if you have a poster that says:

Come and see this hilarious new musical production, straight from New York. Don't miss it!

That's 15 words. By the time they've read that, your precious four-second window of consideration is already over. So let's get trimming.

First off, we can lose the over-used, generic imperatives: *Come and see* and *Don't miss it!*

Next, the redundant words: *this* and *production* (all musicals are productions, and of course you're plugging this one).

Finally, anything that will be assumed by the audience: if you're in Edinburgh, and you're seeing a show from New York, you know it's come *straight from New York*.

Take what's left, rejig the order slightly for flow, and we end up with this:
New York's hilarious new musical.

Same message but 10 words punchier. Which frees up more precious time for potential punters to take in the rest of your poster or flyer.

Now go through the exercise with your own summary blurb – remove the generic, redundant and assumed words, and you'll be left with something tight and strong (basically, the opposite of my abs).

If you apply the same ruthless streamlining to the rest of your blurb, you'll be surprised how pithy you can get it. It's very satisfying.

Smaller

Literally making the words smaller on the page can also be a good option. This is where knowing which elements to prioritise is important. There's a tendency, in trying to attract attention, to MAKE EVERY WORD ON THE PAGE MASSIVE. Unfortunately, by attempting to draw attention to everything, you draw attention to nothing. It's like parents who shout all the time – their kids just tune it out. Making copy smaller is a particularly good option for mandatories like phone numbers, if you have to include them.

As a good rule of thumb, once you've laid out your poster, shrink the words by a font size, or two, to see if it looks more elegant. You can always undo it in a few clicks if you want. Obviously, don't go too far the other way and produce a poster that's only fit for ants (unless that's your incredibly niche target audience!).

You can also try a great suggestion from Paul Arden's book: *It's not how good you are, it's how good you want to be*. Print out a dummy poster, put it at the end of the hall, and see what information you can take from it. Ideally, you should be able to read the performer's name and show title, and perhaps the venue and the dates. That's about it. For any more details, they can come closer, or just look it up on their phone. This is why you should always print a test copy of your poster before you confirm your print run. Text and colours that look fine in Photoshop, or as a digital proof on your phone, can look totally off in real life. Better to discover that by printing one, rather than waiting until you've printed hundreds.

What you can't eliminate, congregate

In other words, look for ways to combine your remaining elements. The 'listings' details (i.e. date, time, venue, price) often work well when grouped together, via a block, a coloured band, or similar holding device. Similarly, if you can group your reviews or star ratings together then people can take them in as a single group. Again, this makes your poster easier to digest, which means more clarity, which means more potential punters.

Also, look out for any unnecessary duplication. For example, if you have two quotes which say 'hilarious', can you lose one, or swap it for a different quote? A good technique, if you have sufficient reviews for it, is to use the reviews to help describe your show. This is delightfully efficient as you can combine two elements (i.e. the quote and the descriptor) into one. Mime stand-up Tape Face used a Simon Cowell quote this way ("A modern Charlie Chaplin"). Comedian and mentalist Doug Segal uses "Imagine if Derren Brown was funny". I've used a longer quote for a similar purpose on the back of one of my flyers.

There is one possible exception to this rule: star ratings. I saw a poster on the tube in London for a revival of *An American Paris*, which said '23 5-star reviews'. While it definitely simplified the layout, and displays an understated confidence, I still felt that seeing a sea of stars would have been more instantly convincing. And although increasing the number of stars may be adding extra elements, since they're all identical, they remain easy to understand at a glance.

Add some air

Once you've got rid of these elements, chances are you will have a few more gaps in your poster. Don't rush to fill them! You don't need to go to Apple-level extremes of minimalism, but a bit of 'white space' lets the picture breathe, and helps to highlight the other elements.

You'll also see during this process why it's good to scamp. The less polished it is, the less it feels like you're destroying something beautiful when you make the necessary changes to improve it. Having said that, if you're truly wedded to your computer, you can also simplify by deleting layers in Photoshop or similar.

Simply – the best

After all that eliminating and combining, you should end up with a poster that is much simpler, and much stronger. If you do a quick Before and After comparison with your first version it's very satisfying. And it's even more satisfying later, when you add your poster to a wall crammed with others, and see your beautifully simple poster shining out. With a few exceptions, it really is a case of less is more.

And that's (almost) a wrap

You've now got a poster. Good job! It should serve you well. And, as you're about to see, converting it to other formats is comparatively easy.

BEYOND POSTERS

Boiling your show down to a simple, powerful poster is hard. But the nice side is, once you've gone through the process, converting it to almost any other medium is relatively easy. I'll cover a few formats, but since they change all the time, just keep these two general principles in mind and you'll be fine.

1. Decide on your hierarchy of information

Rank the different elements of your poster, from the most important to the least. Then make the more important elements more prominent – either bigger or appearing sooner. For example, in the case of a flyer, your show title is very important, so put it nice and big on the front. The venue is less important, so put it smaller, lower down, or on the back.

2. Give increasing degrees of detail

Don't assume that all people will make it to the end of your poster (or flyer, or trailer, etc.). So put the strongest, simplest parts upfront, then add more later. Think of it like a pyramid where the amount of information grows as it goes down.

Flyers

Treat your flyer like a mini poster. While people can spend as long as they want looking in it, when they're overwhelmed with other flyers, you still only have a few seconds to grab their attention. Don't just shrink your poster, as the writing may need adjusting to keep it clearly readable. It's also an idea to shift some of your quotes and other information onto the back of the flyer, so the front looks clean and unbusy, which again will make it stand out.

I tend to keep the essentials of my show – my name, the title, venue, time, top reviews – on the front of my flyer. Others go more minimalist and just have a teaser image or headline on the front.

For instance, Darren Walsh had a flyer for his 2018 show which just had 'Do you like puns?' on the front. I think this is a smart approach for his punderful show as, like pineapple on pizza, people have strong opinions on puns, so it makes sense to filter out the haters and leave it for the lovers like me.

Who knows which approach is more effective? I'd love to see someone do an A/B test with two versions of their flyer, but until then, just pick one approach and go with that.

Stick a short version of your blurb on the back. And I mean short. The following structure has worked well for me: Start with a single sentence that sums up your show. Then, as a second paragraph, add a couple more sentences expanding on what the show contains. Finally, as a third paragraph, give a few reasons why you and your show are objectively good (sell-out shows, reviews, etc.).

Here's an example from *When Magic & Science Collide*:

Amazing tricks inspired by astounding science.

Oliver Meech meddles with forces we barely understand, in a comedy magic show for the QI generation. It's the natural selection!

2 sell-out Edinburgh runs. "My jaw hit the floor" BBC Radio. "Hilarious" Buxton Fringe.

If your venue is hard to find then you may wish to put a map on the back, but now everyone has Google Maps, I generally wouldn't use up your space with it.

Online banners

Treat these like posters, but even simpler, as people's attention is so fleeting. The name of the show, maybe one review, the dates, and maybe the venue and time, though if it clicks through to your show listing you may not need it. Again, less is more.

When you have a rotating banner, have the essentials come up early, or consider having them in a bar along the bottom throughout. People often spend just a few seconds on each page before clicking through to another, so most won't even get to see the fourth frame of your banner.

Posters in different formats

Portrait, landscape, square, random T-shapes – sometimes you'll have to rejig your poster to fit a different format. It can be a pain, but just use your common sense and keep the important parts prominent, and it'll work out. The need for different formats is also something to keep in mind when planning your show image. When possible, shoot a bit wider than you need, so you can crop the resulting photo in different ways. If that ship has sailed, then you can often add in a bit more background on Photoshop, which is one argument for having a plain (or easily duplicated) background.

YES, BUT...

As Robert Burns (and then Eddie Izzard) have noted, the best laid plans of mice and men often go astray.

There's the calm, ordered plan that you read about in books, then the messy, stressy reality that you live in. So here are some tips on what to do if you find yourself up Fringe creek.

Yes, but what if I have no photos?

This happened to me with my first solo show. I got my dates muddled and suddenly discovered that I had to submit my show image to a printed programme in a couple of days, while I was away on holiday in America. Aaaargh! I decided to go for a simple silhouette drawing instead. I drew a quick scamp, emailed my talented graphic novelist chum Karrie Fransman back in the UK, she drew it up properly, and I was sorted.

Other options:

- If you know an illustrator, turn to them
- Find an illustrator or graphic designer on a website like Fiverr and have them knock something up for you
- Go deliberately unpolished – take a photo on a passport photo machine and use that, complete with the white border
- Take a photo on your phone and play with some different tints

Yes, but what if I have no reviews?

If you don't have any for your current (or previous) shows, then see if there are any about you as a performer that you can use, like this:

"Oliver Meech ("amazing" SomeBlog) brings his new show 'Unprepared' to..."

If you don't have that, see if you can swiftly organise a living-room preview. I didn't invent this idea, but invite some friends over, give them some food, and do your show for them. Afterwards, say outright that you are looking for nice quotes to help sell the show, so if they enjoyed it, please can they post a short review online. If they're stuck, ask them to sum up the show in three words, which should result in some lovely, pithy superlatives which you can use. You can now quote them on your poster.

For completeness, there's also the option of doing an obviously made up quote.

E.g. *"The best show ever made"* My Mum.

It's been done quite a lot, so I'd try to avoid it, but it's an option. Actually, for my *Time Warper* show, I had two proper quotes, then one saying "Amazing" from Henry VIII. Yes, it was silly, but it did at least fit with the show's theme.

Yes, but what if I have no money?

See if you can do a skill swap with someone else. Or try Fiverr.com – a cheap entry-level designer may still be more skilled than you. Or do it yourself. I ended up laying out my posters, to keep costs low. While it wasn't ideal, the end results were effective, in part because the ideas for my show images were inherently attention-grabbing. This is another good reason to devote the majority of your time to coming up with a good idea for your show image.

Yes, but what if I have no time?

It's amazing what you can get done in 24 hours when you really need to. And I've always found fellow performers to be very supportive. So, put out a distress call and get hustling.

In the same way that done is better than perfect, almost anything is better than nothing. A show with no image should be avoided if at all possible, if only because it gives people trying to narrow down their options an easy way to dismiss your show. So do whatever you can in the time available. Remember, you don't usually need to finalise your poster until after you've submitted your show image, so if worse comes to worst, just submit the best image of your face you have, then use that image in your subsequent poster, when you come to create it.

If, despite your best efforts, you somehow miss the deadline and have a generic image, then don't lose heart. Just refocus on making a compelling poster and flyer and throw yourself into plugging your show on the day – for every person who plans in advance what they're going to see, there's someone else who plumps for whoever hands them the best flyer that day.

OUTRO

Well done for making it to the end. Hopefully you've now gone from 'Aaargh!' to 'Ahhh'. Creating a good poster may not be quick or easy, but it's totally worth it. You can feel rightly proud to have put something good out into the world, and hopefully sold more tickets in the process. Now go forth and have a great show!

SPREAD THE WORD

If you enjoyed this book then I'd be really grateful if you could give me a good review on Amazon, tell your performer friends, or mention it online. Thanks!

ACKNOWLEDGEMENTS

Big thanks to these good people for helping make this book happen:

Ruth Meech for her sterling support and for giving her time to free up mine for writing.

Karrie Fransman for being a brilliant sounding board for all my creative projects.

Rebecca Taylor for her eagle-eyed proofing. Any errors that remain are mine.

Grzegorz Japoł for all his efforts at making the design process effortless for me.

And finally, you for buying and reading it.

GET IN TOUCH

One of my favourite things about being a performer is all the wonderful, warm people I get to meet.

So I'd love to hear from you with any comments, questions, suggestions or invitations.

Get in touch via my website: **olivermeech.com**

I also occasionally offer one-on-one advice on creating show posters. If you're interested, drop me a line and we'll go from there.

I can't wait to see what you create!

APPENDIX – USEFUL RESOURCES

Edinburgh Fringe:

- *How to Produce, Perform and Write an Edinburgh Fringe Comedy Show* by Ian Fox
  Ian's a top bloke, and he's been there, done that and bought the Fringe t-shirt.

- *The Fringe Guide to Selling A Show*
  Available at edfringe.com. It covers all the essentials. Good for common-sense tips that are commonly overlooked.

- *The Edinburgh Fringe Survival Guide: How to Make Your Show a Success* by Mark Fisher
  A helpful primer of all the things to consider, with tips from lots of Edinburgh Fringe experts.

- *Laughing Horse Free Festival* (freefestival.co.uk)
  A great way to do Edinburgh without spending a

fortune. I've done a few runs with them and always enjoyed the experience.

- *Just The Tonic* (justthetonic.com)
Another great venue group that I've performed with several times. They offer a helpful mix of pricing models, and treat their performers well.

Advertising:

- *Creative Advertising* by Mario Pricken
A smorgasbord of creative ads from around the world, categorised by creative technique. While they're for brands rather than shows, a lot of the same techniques can be applied.

- *The Advertising Concept Book: Think Now, Design Later* by Pete Barry
A similar yet different book, filled with interesting ads, all scamped (i.e. sketched), to keep the focus purely on the idea.

Design:

- *The Non-Designer's Design Book* by Robin Williams
An excellent book with oodles of examples, to help train your eye.

Freelance designer sites:

- *Fiverr* (fiverr.com)
A solid starting point, with designers ranging from cheap to a bit pricier.

- *99designs* (99designs.com)
More expensive, but to some degree, you get what you pay for.

Printers:

- *The Fringe Shop* (thefringeshop.co.uk)
  Very experienced at producing print for the fringe.

- *Instantprint* (instantprint.co.uk)
  More automated, so good for when you just need standard posters and flyers produced quickly and cheaply.

Brainstorming:

- *The Writer's Block: 786 Ideas To Jump-start Your Imagination* by Jason Rekulak
  Written for writers, but many of the prompts work just as well for creating posters.

Copywriting:

- *Copyblogger* (copyblogger.com)
  While mainly aimed at bloggers and content marketers, they have good free blogs and ebooks with general advice about writing.